# The
# Rock-n-Roll
# Coloring Book
## (volume I)

## by Andrew Szava-Kovats

# True Age Media

POB 9701, Lowell, MA 01852
www.TrueAgeMedia.com

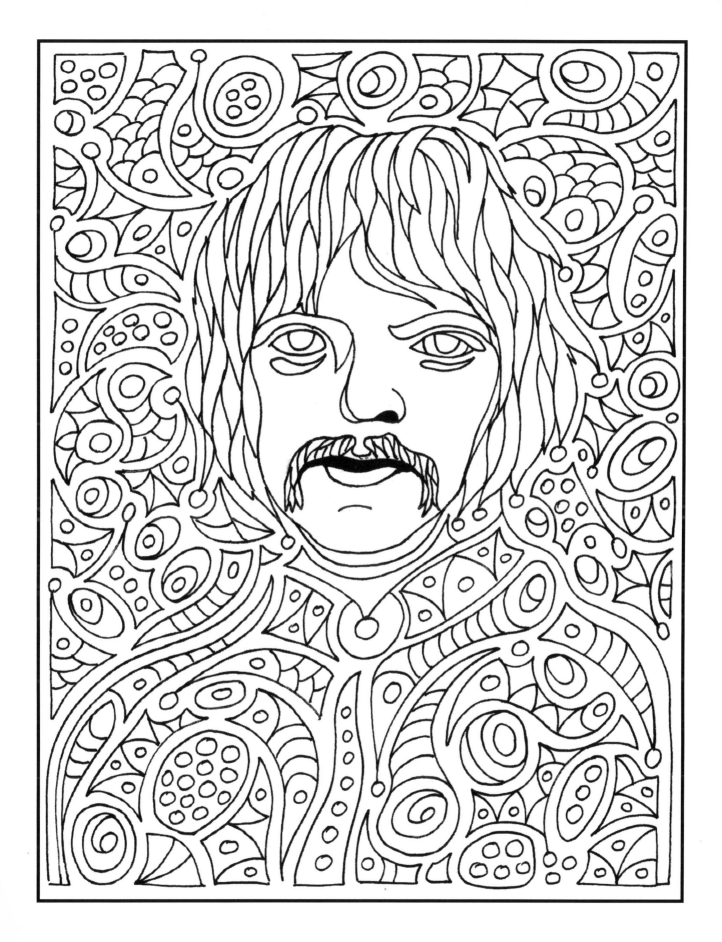

# The Portraits:

1. Elvis Presley (1935-1977)
2. Chuck Berry
3. Buddy Holly (1936-1959)
4. Jerry Lee Lewis
5. Bob Dylan
6. John Lennon (1940-1980)
7. Paul McCartney
8. George Harrison (1943-2001)
9. Ringo Starr
10. Mick Jagger
11. Janis Joplin (1943-1970)
12. Jimi Hendrix (1942-1970)
13. Jim Morrison (1943-1971)
14. Eric Clapton
15. Pete Townsend - "The Who"
16. Grace Slick - "Jefferson Airplane"
17. Gerry Garcia (1942-1995) - "The Grateful Dead"
18. Lou Reed (1942-2013) - "Velvet Underground"
19. Joni Mitchell
20. Graham Nash
21. David Crosby
22. Neil Young
23. Chris Squire (1948-2015) - "Yes"
24. Steve Howe - "Yes"
25. David Gilmore - "Pink Floyd"
26. Ian Anderson - "Jethro Tull"
27. Steven Tyler - "Aerosmith"
28. Carlos Santana
29. Frank Zappa - "The Mothers of Invention"
30. Stevie Nicks - "
31. Brian May - "Queen"
32. Freddy Mercury (1941-1991) - "Queen"
33. Iggy Pop - "Iggy & the Stooges"
34. David Bowie
35. Brian Eno - "Roxy Music"
36. Bryan Ferry - "Roxy Music"

37. Ann & Nancy Wilson - "Heart"
38. Patti Smith
39. Debbie Harry - "Blondie"
40. Angus Young - "AC/DC"
41. Joan Jett - "The Runaways"
42. Joey Ramone - "The Ramones"
43. Johnny Rotten - "The Sex Pistols"
44. Sid Vicious - "The Sex Pistols"
45. Siouxsie - "Siouxsie & the Banshees"
46. Robert Smith - "The Cure"
47. Bono - "U2"
48. Kate Pierson - "The B52s"
49. Natelie Merchant - "10,000 Maniacs"
50. Wendy O Williams - "The Plasmatics"

Made in the USA
Middletown, DE
18 December 2017